#UntitledOne

#UntitledOne

Neu! Reekie! Publishing #1

Edited by
KEVIN WILLIAMSON and MICHAEL PEDERSEN

Polygon

First published in Great Britain in 2015 Neu! Reekie! Publishing
and by Polygon, an imprint of Birlinn Ltd.

Birlinn Ltd
West Newington House
10 Newington Road
Edinburgh
EH9 1QS

www.polygonbooks.co.uk

ISBN 978 1 84697 334 5
eBook ISBN 978 0 85790 866 7

British Library Cataloguing-in-Publication Data
A catalogue record for this book is available
on request from the British Library.

Design and typesetting by Gerry Cambridge
Printed and bound in Great Britain by TJ International Ltd, Padstow, Cornwall

Contents

Acknowledgments & Thanks

We would like to thank all the artists who've contributed to this publication and everyone who has helped make this baby fly. Special thanks go to Alison, Vikki and everyone at Polygon for their vision, patience and persistence. To Gerry Cambridge for his indefatigible work on design and typesetting: a true font of all knowledge. To our backers and sponsors at Creative Scotland and John Dewar & Sons, plus Bréon at Dreamtower for helping keep the show on the road. To Summerhall for the continued support in so many different ways. And to everyone who's come to our events as performers or audience. Print is important but when push comes to shove it's all about the live happenings. Finally we'd like to express our thanks to everyone who's helped spread the word, helped out at events—especially Gavin and Mike who've been with us from the start—or helped connect us with so many interesting artists and venues. You know who you are and your support has been very much appreciated.

Some of these poems may have appeared previously in a variety of splendid books, chapbooks, magazines, journals, e-zines and blogs; to these publications of good taste we pay fond thanks. The necessary permissions for their publication in *#UntitledOne* have been sought out by the individual authors —please contact us for further details or with queries regarding any specific work. Hat tipped to independent literature (specifically that of Scottish stock).

Kevin & Michael
Edinburgh
May 2015

Twitter: @neureekie
Pusbook: www.facebook.com/neureekie
Tumblr: www.neureekie.com

#UntitledOne—Mission Statement

'The future can not be trusted. The moment of truth is now. And more and more it will be poetry, rather than prose, that receives this truth.'

—John Berger, The Hour of Poetry

IN THE BEGINNING was the word.

Neu! Reekie! was launched in January 2011, in Edinburgh's Old Town, down a dimly lit alley off the Canongate. Trunk's Close leads to the home of Scottish Book Trust which, for our purposes, was nicely tucked away from prying eyes and the Friday-night hordes. There were to be no paid adverts. No hype. We made that clear from the start. Word of mouth plus bare-bone details to local zines.

I met Michael the previous summer when we shared a poetry stage in Glasgow. He claims his interest was aroused because I performed Robert Burns poems wearing a shell suit and wrapround sunglasses. Said it was what Rabbie would've worn if he'd been alive today. I can't remember ever having a shell suit but once we got talking and drinking we got plotting and planning and decided to launch a regular poetry night in the Scottish capital.

I took a bit of persuasion at first. I hadn't organised any literature nights since Rebel Inc. called it a day at the end of 2000. My first impression of Michael was that he was keen as mustard, had a bit of swagger about him, and was quite young. A lot younger than me. In his mid-twenties. That was the clincher. Last thing I wanted to do was organise poetry events for middle-aged farts like me.

Michael knew a lot of musicians and bands. There was a gang of ragamuffin troubadors he hung out with who performed under the name Emelle. Three of them, including singer Craig Lithgow, were brothers. They were exciting to watch, they wrote their own songs, and they had a youthful swagger about them too. We booked them for the first night and after that kept them on as our 'house band' to finish off each show.

My special interest was in animation. Short animated films for adults. The final two Rebel Inc. shows, ten years earlier, mixed spoken word with animation. It was a format that worked and one I'd wanted to explore further if the chance came along.

Poetry and animation. Animation and poetry. The two were made for each other. The brilliant Czech filmmaker, Jan Švankmajer, one of the masters of stop-motion animation, understood the overlap: 'I am still convinced that poetry is the foundation of all art forms, that it stands in their centre, and all the rest are but means for grasping it. That also applies to animation. The means are interchangeable.'

Now into its fifth year Neu! Reekie! is based at the Summerhall Arts complex and has organised over seventy of these cultural showcases, on three continents, featuring spoken word, animation and live music. Other eclectic elements are thrown into the mix, just to see what happens.

Each show is conceptualised as a 2–3-hour experience rather than simply curated or hosted. There is no dead time at our shows. From the moment the audience walks in until we bring the curtain down, each event is a happening, planned within its own time and physical space, and lovingly constructed, piece by piece, the way a composer approaches a symphony. The art of juxtaposition and surprise.

Now here we are in 2015. It's taken me fifteen years to put my toe back into the book publishing waters. Since I was last involved the terrain has changed greatly. And not much for the better. But poetry still matters. Books still matter. Art still matters. More so than ever. The barbarians are at the gates.

News feeds, Twitter feeds, Facebook feeds—all tumble before our eyes like attention-seeking Niagaras of distraction. The Infotainment Skim. But books are solid. David Hockney called it right in *Secret Knowledge*: 'You bring your own time to a book. It is not imposed, as with television or film. With a book you can stop to think something through.'

#UntitledOne is the first published document from Neu! Reekie! It features thirty-one poets and twenty-one bands/musicans. Almost all of them have performed live at Neu! Reekie! They are who we are. The only poet included in this anthology who hasn't performed at Neu! Reekie! is the late Paul Reekie. Paul died in June 2010 at the age of forty-eight. He is a guiding spirit and Neu! Reekie! is named after him.

Enjoy.

Kevin Williamson
May 2015

Adelle Stripe

Sacred Heart

on a train, through the fog, where the sun was the moon
and boats laid asleep on the silver rink marsh
where church spires were strangled by dead tree silhouettes
i listened to the murmur of sorrowful songs

the flickering light was my own dream machine
fingertips numb i pictured verlaine
and walked over cobbles (past dogshit and bottles)
up steps to a view through antique snickleways

this was our journey, hands tracing hangmen
a hundred *i love yous* scratched on blue paint
crumbs of old pastry scattered on tables
a thick russian hat kept the cold from my face

under pale domes of the cracked french cathedral
(an old taj mahal dripping wax on pigalle)
conversation distilled into transparent pearls
my words dry as ice condensed in the sunlight

i tapped on the handrails in vatican gift shops,
where icons in gold were sold for a steal
to tourists, as penance, coins forming small mountains
a new den of thieves in a black flag bastille

a ring on my hand, hematite, fitted tight
followed the shape of an archangel's feet
where requiem's silence was spiked by stilettos
the sound ricocheted from the black stained glass peaks

past bistros, bookshops, or cafes, where old men
leaned against heaters smoking gitanes
you pulled on my patch gloves, rubbed on my hands
and bought me éclairs by an old peepshow stand

in only five hours, a snapshot in time
walking like ghosts of a decadent past
without a direction, we stared at manaras;
blood, spit and sawdust—a wintertime fast.

Adelle Stripe

Big Weekend

you were the cock of the north white jeans shiny versace belt not a knock off from leeds market not for you no snakeskin patrick cox loafers benson and hedges romany skin back in '96 i remember the night of brian's wake eleven hours drinking lager you and me and chris—brian's son—they lived next door to us the family who always shouted and let their dog shit in our garden chris was pretty fucked up that night brian had hung himself from the stair rafters and it wasn't chris' fault but he thought it was he thought it was all because of the court case his fault he drove his dad to it and you and him were friends from way back you were bad children always riding round the estate on stolen bikes beating other kids up you were boys whose mothers loved them too much but the night of brian's wake we were all back at harold hick court in simon's flat simon with the tiny pinned pupils we listened to what's the story morning glory all of us stinking from daytime drinking and you and chris were being boisterous teasing each other i went for a piss in the dirty bathroom and when i came back you and him were fighting on the carpet the two of you smashing punches into each other and as always chris took it too far and broke a bottle stabbing the raw green glass into your hand which sprayed red all over your white jeans you were yelling at him and the rest of the lads had to pin chris down he said he was going to fucking kill you i pulled you towards the sink and pushed your messy hand under the tap shouting for sellotape and binding your hand with it cutting the pulsing blood off you said thank you and gave me a small peck on the side of my face then a few of the lads got out small sealy bags and started smoking brown powder off tin foil like an origami bird all silvery and bright in the dark doomy flat and you smoked some of it up through an empty biro and i knew things were going a bit far but i couldn't help watching and felt a bit sick from the musty fish smell and i didn't take any because i was too scared that i'd throw up all over myself but i watched you go quiet eyes all watery the very same look that lots of boys had on sunday afternoons so i laid on the sofa pretending to sleep and watched your lion face gouch on the sticky kitchen lino chris was sharing needles with my school friends danny and ant and another called dave making tourniquets from their knock-off gucci belts and right there at 5am it struck me if i didn't pack my bags and leave for somewhere better i too would be dragged into the same helpless hole that all of you had dug because the only difference between a rut and a grave is the depth.

3

Aidan Moffat

#lessthanthree

GF, ABT our <3:
ur my own CC, OMFG;
we're NSFW all nite—
FFS, u <3 me rite!
IDK WTF
i wld do if u evr left—
FYI, prbly i'd die
b/c ILY, just ICYMI
(n BTW, b4 u came,
<3 was *just a game*)

so i EML these wrds 2 whr u r—
i hope their not TL n u DR;
n pls pls LMK if u wont stay—
n if its tru, i'll STFU.

Aidan Moffat

Scene from a Saturday, 1996

INT. BUSY, LIVELY PUB. EARLY EVENING.

GAZ and TONY sit side by side at a worn, wooden table,
finishing pints as I arrive. My chair grates against the
floor as I pull it out to join them and say—

> ME:
> Alright?
>> GAZ:
> Yeah.
>>> TONY:
> Alright.

They don't look up. I sit down.

> GAZ (TO TONY):
> Tell you what, I'd shag at least
> ninety per cent of the birds in here.

> TONY (TO GAZ):
> Nah, man—seventy, seventy-five
> maybe. Have a look at this
> though! Nine o'clock!

TONY'S eyes target something behind me.

> GAZ (TO TONY):
> Eh? It's just gone seven.

> TONY (TO GAZ):
> No, it's where she's standing.
> Like on planes in the war. Fit
> bird at nine o'clock !

GAZ (TO TONY):
Ah, right. What way's twelve?

TONY (TO GAZ):
Straight ahead. Fucking idiot.

GAZ points his hand straight ahead and winds it back to 9.
He finds THE BIRD, his eyebrows raising as he nods in
approval.

ME:
Drinks?

TONY:
Lager, yeah.

GAZ just shakes his empty glass at me.

Clare Pollard

Los Indignados

Your hands are useless.
We do not need them
to knead bread, to thread,
plant seeds, enter data.

Your arms are useless.
We don't need muscles
to lift or drag or build.
We have margins.

Your legs are useless.
We do not need you
to march to battles;
ring doorbells.

Your voice is useless.
It is too expensive—
educated and with rights,
it won't repeat by rote.

Your mind is useless.
We have search-engines.
Post images for free,
be glad of the opportunity.

This is austerity.
We have cameras to see—
eyes are useless; worse.
You are the surplus.

Clare Pollard

Suffer

Your negative thoughts might harm the foetus
and you might abort the foetus or think about aborting the foetus
or just not be that maternal
and you got pissed at that wedding and cava can harm the foetus.

You might inhale or eat a soft-boiled egg or brim a boiling bath or have more
than one point five cups of coffee.

You might wake to find you slept on your back or your right (or is it left?) side.

You might slip or run or lift or weed or dye your hair or use most household
products.

You might forget your folic acid
and you're overweight or underweight or thirty eight
and that elderflower pressé you just treated yourself to at the bar can cause
gestational diabetes
and you didn't have the downs test or had the test
and you've not joined yoga or hypnobirthing
and stress can harm the foetus.

You might not have bought a birthing ball.

You might opt for an epidural.

You might squeal for the fucking drugs or they might have to cut you open.

You might have no milk or sour milk or mastitis
or loathe the way your nipples fizz; how they squirt
like a clown's flower-brooch.

You might look at her and feel underwhelmed.

You might drop her or break that delicate neck or that terrible vulnerable pit
in the back of her skull.

You might overheat or swaddle or bring her in your bed or fall asleep whilst feeding.

You might let your hand lose contact with the baby in the bath
or leave the pram a moment
or leave her in the car-seat or not strap her in the car-seat properly.

You might own an envious cat.

You might leave a window open or a door or let her play outside unsupervised like paedo-bait or fox-bait and the tabloids will imply things.

You might have blinds and sockets and stairs
and a pond or know someone with a pond.

Also you might let her watch too much *CBeebies* or have a dummy or cheap shoes or food with too much salt or MMR or pink plastic princess crap or be spoiled.

You might make inappropriate comments about her weight.

You might give her your nose.

You might give her poor hand–eye coordination or a flaw in the chambers of her heart.

Also letting her 'cry it out' can damage her brain
and you have a routine or no routine
and are probably yummy or slummy—
silting up cafés with your Bugaboo and NCT buddies
overthinking latching
or abandoning her to zitty sitters
so you can get drunk and be clumsy or lurid or not there.

You might be cold and hard like all those bags of expressed milk that tumble out
and hurt your feet each time you open the freezer.

You might be too much, too smothery: eating her toes and pressing moist desperate kisses on her tiny struggling head all *ga-ga-goo-goo-mummy-stinks-an-ickle-bit-of-milkypoo* as you sink into the sicky sofa; the bad-meat leak still slop-bucketing your knickers (you're so torn it hurts to fart even).

You might not have washed-up or opened the curtains and you're watching *Loose Women* you're so pathetic, pathetic!

You might have sex within her earshot and she'll think you're being stabbed
and be traumatised or jealous or Electra
or her daddy will divorce you or dick around
because you slacked off from perineal massage or pelvic floor exercises
and you've lost your libido
and he saw the business end.

Also you might have a career.

You'll probably be in a high-powered meeting when she says her first word
which will be 'mama' to the nanny
or you might be unable to afford a nanny
or she won't take the bottle or they won't let you go part-time or will make you redundant
and you'll throw yourself into bake-offs making cupcakes so sophisticated they express your inner death
and did you forget to sign onto that nursery waiting list two years before she was born?
And you say you haven't been to *Little Movers*?

The health visitor might say she isn't gaining weight:
her pencil point wounding the chart in the wrong place.

She might call in social services.

They might find out you're alone or on benefits or medication or have damp and take your baby.

You might deserve it.

You might smack her or beat her or stub fags out on her succulent little thighs or lock her under stairs or chain her to a bed or let her sit in her own shit all day

You might sell her or pimp her or mutilate her genitals
or expose her on a mountainside or flush her down a sewage pipe
or leave her with an 'uncle' or a priest.
or touch her or not touch her
or take photos.

Also you might watch her starve because you brought her into a world with
finite resources and an unsustainable rate of population growth.

You might watch a fly dance on her eye.

You might let a celebrity adopt her.

You might watch her die of a treatable disease.

You might watch her die of an untreatable disease in a kids' ward with murals of
Dumbo or *In the Night Garden*.

You might live in a war zone and be unable to protect her.

You might not live in a good catchment area.

You might live in a poor catchment area and be unwilling to run a church tom-
bola to protect her.

You might not be able to stop climate change.

You might not be able to offer her hope.

You might smother her then gas yourself or hold her and jump off a cliff or use
that knife, *that* knife, the one you looked at too long in the kitchen this morning
even though it goes without saying you don't want to never could.

You might lie awake at 3 a.m. listening for her breath
or not love her enough or love her so much it's a sickness, it's sick.

You might go mad.

David Kinloch

A Portrait of the Author on the Verge of Sleep

Legs twist in echo of the foetal
Slump I struck within the parlour
Of my mother's womb.

Cut me some light again!
This skellie-ankled shut-eye
Is the opposite of sleep.

Place your legs beside each other
On the sheet. The light is off.
The night is in. Hark! My lover's

Nasal strip has prinked his nostrils
Up. But that delicate Bugatti buzz
Will soon become the whole of Britain

Fracked to kingdom come. I resign myself
With Mallarmean vigour to the dark
This verse defends

And start to think: don't describe,
Ekphrastic wits dictate. Enact the art
Your poetry depicts. Can you spell out

A snore?—sleep's selfie taken in total
Ignorance of itself?—I switch on my iPhone's
Movie app so I can replay the night's loud score;

He'll call me 'bitch', repay the compliment.
But there! A moment's silence puddles
In your mind and you drift briefly to the verge . . .

Verge or 'verge' in French is a proper noun
For penis. And thoughts of those assail attempts
At slumber. A bestiary of dicks and rods

And other monosyllables prick up their snouts.
Ah God! Think of the literature
That has come from dreams and then there's

This. How bland the dark is; like
Gay marriage; about to cover all
With its pall of dense similitude,

Snuff out the handy tea lights
I used to hold to tit clamps
Or warm the odd Prince Albert.

Soon the stubborn bachelor
Will be looked at with askance:
Where are your adopted kids?

Your husband?—an Old Norse
Word that replaced Old English
'Wer' who was the mate of 'Wif'.

—(A sad acoustic loss for English
Poetry, the online dictionary
Astutely notes.)—Forgive me:

I know a wild Venn diagram
Where the oval buns
Of civil partnership and wedlock

Kiss each other's sweet
Spots in connubial bliss. Yet there are
Rows on the same spreadsheet

As yet uncolonised; a space,
Similarly pendulous perhaps,
Or just the just effect of light.

Look closely: you may detect
The shadow of the only cupid's
Arrow worth a candle:

With Zeno's name upon it,
Always streaking to the target,
Never there but never still.

Douglas Dunn

Botanics

Muticoloured clothespegs on the line
Are tiny tropical birds hanging upside down.
Their songs are all imaginary.
The tree peony's a candelabrum,
Botanical flame-holder. Maples speak
Native American languages, a eucalypt
Aboriginal Australian, Pieris
A secret tongue of the forest. Magnolia—
Which I don't have although a neighbour does—
Discusses Missisippi in a Dixie drawl.
Ranks of *en garde* gladioli speak
Byzantine Greek, roses Babylonish
And other floral tongues, while quince
Talks Arabic, and an azalea is
A chatterbox in Hindi and Chinese.
Lilies whisper across continents
In secret, erotic dialects
That baffle botanical philologists.
Crab-apple—good for jelly—it speaks
Weathered and salty Atlantic lingos,
Survivors' syntax. Spare a thought
For currents, strawberry, raspberry, gooseberry,
Indigenous desserts, mother-made jam,
For lilacs, elder, and the evergreens,
For the big library of tree-poetry
In botany's symphonic chorus.

Douglas Dunn

Transport in Madagascar

Magnified, the engraving shows
A pith-helmeted European sitting
On a chair slung between two poles,
Two bearers at each end, headed
Towards an almost-mediaeval skyline—
Tananarive. Gibbon describes
'Transport in Madagascar', Yvert
Transport en filanzane. No irony,
Either way. The White Man's Burden
Involves being carried to the city.
All five are faceless with their backs
To us, as if the engraver sensed
Two kinds of shame, the conquerors'
And conquereds'. Turning the pages
Shows a mounted General Galliéni—
Stamps give blue, orange, magenta
And green horses, without anyone
Thinking it's a modernist stunt,
A horse by Picasso or Paul Muldoon—
Followed by zebus (long-horned buffalos),
A Saklava chief (very fine in brown
And scarlet, finer in deep magenta
And brown), and local pulchritude,
Barely nubile, a green girl, a scarlet girl.

And the strange flora, ravenala
(Travellers' trees), pachypodes,
Remote, resplendent botany
On an island that's neither African
Nor Asian, but Indian Ocean's,
Not knowing which way to turn.
My kind of place, Carruthers.
Hitler's theorists thought Madagascar
The perfect spot for dumping Europe's Jews.
Luck of the Legion led his men

Through its jungles in *The Eagle*.
Such reading is risible now,
Clean, decent, and educational.
Ditto the wonderful *Wizard*,
Adventure and *The Children's Newspaper*.
Far too good for this world.
Why should they be impossible now?
The innocent wonder of postage stamps—
The glimpse of the far, far away . . .
Now they mortify the flesh
With cost and rarity, elusiveness,
With bids at auctions, the pains
And pleasures of obsession, sore,
Anxious acquisitiveness of paper,
Spendthrift squalor, a touch of love
In such rancid extravagances.
Can childhood be rebought?
Can there be fresh starts, and helped by
An innocent expenditure?
Is it a quest for innocence?

I love this remote expertise, far
From the concerns of so-called 'friends'
Interested in 'gigs', applause, and fees.
A poetical philatelist,
I spend my evenings in a mist
Through which a hundred colours weave
Their shades and little pictures, pure
In their beauty, and also in
Their useless, lovely information.
Is this my 'poetic'? My 'aesthetic'?
The silent, the lovely, the useless?—
Or the useful that's become useless.
The sun sets. A beautiful day grows dark
As I lift Madagascar in my hands.

Douglas Dunn

A Basket of Apples

In memory of Barbara Murray

I see them still as a painting by Peploe
Or even a lesser colourist on a good day,
These fruits of early autumn's visible taste.
A memory, but it's not one of sorrow.
Offered to all—'Don't let them go to waste'—
Outside your office door, as if you'd said
'It's not all work, you know. Take a good bite.
Relish slowly.' That was your gift to us,
An annual present, freely given away,
Out of consideration, out of kindness.
Your country apples savoured of East Neuk light!
Apples, teaching, scholarship, and care—
Commonplace fruits, except you placed them there,
Their green, their gold, their yellow, bronze and red.

Emer Martin

Underground

The Incomplete 3-Minute History of Ireland

I was going underground. Under my life. Under the country. Under the barley. Under the potatoes. Under the churches. Under the lunatic asylums. Under the cow shit. Under the wild primroses on the hedges. Under the schools. Under Bridget's cloak. Under the bed where I gave birth to my twins. Under the courts that stole my children.

Under the chieftains and druids who sliced our son's nipples and stuck them face down in the Iron Age bog. Under Patrick's staff that pinned me to the bed where the doctors held me down and attached electrodes to my head. Under my womb madness. Under the connivance of monks that took our stories and twisted them into their own.

Under the Vikings who plundered our treasures. Under the betrayers, the snitches, the deal makers that welcomed our enemies to the shore. Under the Normans pouring tar at us from their freezing green zone castles. Under the flight of the Earls who left us to ourselves, what a joke, as if we stood on the edge of the cliffs with hankies waving them off, poor miserable peasants that we were. Come back, oh nobility, and fuck us again.

Under Cromwell who scoured the land of us and banished us to stony windy wet mountains where even the sheep lost their footing and plunged into the sea. Under the Brits who beat our language out of us. Under the landlords who put us out on the soft side of the road. Under the world where the fairies are. Where the limbo babies' tiny skeletons still cage their earthstuck souls; because heaven wouldn't open to them. Under the tangled roots of imported trees. Under the huge machines that stripped the bogs empty. Under the world where the fairies are. Under the music that squeaked out of the boxes, the air that rushes from flutes, the bang of the drum. Under the low lying ever thickening clouds. Under the blight. Under the boats that shipped corn to England. Under the deck of the coffin ships.

Under the people of 1916 who were what, but children of the starved who crawled out of the West. Under Páidraig Pearse's gammy eye and bad poetry. Under the stone yard in Kilmainam Gaol, where they tied the wounded James Connelly to a chair and shot him. Under the Black and Tans. Under the constant grey sky. Under failed negotiations of poor leadership.

Under each other now. Under the Blue Shirts. Under Beal na Blaith. Under Archbishop McQuaid rasping in DeValera's ear as they made plans for us. Under the poets who ordered us to open the door without giving us the key. Under the picture of the Sacred Heart offering us his inedible organ pressed with thorns. Under the singers who made us shiver but would not warm us. Under the endless decades of the rosary. Under the museums that hid the Sile na Gigs from us.

Under the pricks of self-loathing men who stuck it into us and condemned us as dirty with their juice. Under the Virgin Mary who will one day show no mercy to the child in Granard. She is the one and only, the holy and immaculate virgin that renders all us mothers whores. Under the cassocks of the bishops and cardinals and the popes with their useless cocks like ticking metronomes marking out time until the chickens come home to roost.

Under Ben Bulben. Under the endless verses of rebel songs. Under the drink. The poitin that could turn you raw blind, the Guinness that blackens your shite, the uisce baithe that bursts your liver. Under the fierce watch of the bad nuns who ate their sandwiches and drank their lemonade as the starved children in their care collected turf for their parlours. Under the solicitors, the guards, the school principals, the doctors, the bank managers, the decent people of Ireland who you need to sign for your passport.

Under the thud and hum of the laundries. Under the heaps of banned books from exiled scribblers. Under the shoeless bloody feet of slave children in the obscene care of the church and state. Uncounted lives melted like snow off a ditch. Under the fairy forts in Meath, the hag stones in Beara, the disappeared Georgian buildings.

Under the IRA, the RUC, the INLA, the UVF, the SAS, MI6. Under the bombs, the assassinations, the murders, the kneecapping, the man who was shot dead outside his house last night. Under the toll roads that they built to slice through the Neolithic underworld that they refused to understand. Under the tribunals, the confessions, the recessions, the depressions. The brown bags of money under tables.

Under the triple chins of the dazed fat creatures who sold us to the IMF and went creeping off with huge pensions. Under the heroine, the flats, the dirty canals, the coke come-downs, the cathedral like shopping centres, the developers, the bankers, the crap ugly buildings standing empty, the unlandscaped blank green spaces in the sprawling housing estates built on floodplains, the unsignposted roundabouts. Which way now? Which way now?

Under your shrivelled breast, oh hag, that I sucked and sucked, but it was too late to come to you for nourishment so dried out were you with our neglect. And when you cried out in pain it was only black crows that squeezed out of your tear ducts and flew at me as I lay in your embrace and all of these hag crows plucked chunks out of me, until dismembered, I was taken off inside the black noise of the flock in small separate pieces and squawkingly digested and shat out onto the forest floor, and eaten by insects, and inside these creepy crawlies, under the canopy of trees, when the insects died and dried up, the soil of this land took me for what it could suck out of me which of course wasn't much by then, was it oh Ireland?

George Gunn

Wellington

It is as if they wear red coats
the regiments of lodge-pole pines
which guard the banks of the River Borgie
because they are casualties now
twisted & broken in the rough artillery
of commercial forestry
as if Wellington has used them
to cover a hasty retreat
during the close run thing of Waterloo
I see as I walk battlefield smoke
beneath the castle of Bheinn Loaghall
I hear the screams of dying soldiers
& witness the commoditised blood
of timber & men soak into the peat

George Gunn

Wound

Take this wound that I offer you
keep it close & love it well
for the storm may run at Faraid
the surf turn white Loch Eriboll
but no wind can blow an organised people
across the unknowable ocean
or drown their history in the swell

we are cut & yes we bleed
but we are time & headland & will heal
forging our strength by Naver & Torrisdale
tempering our own steel for our own knife

so drink from this cup
the sea on your lip will tingle
the vast democracy of life

Helen Ivory

My Two Fathers

When my father removes his skin
he steps to one side and tidies
the old skin away with a dustpan and brush.

He wants nothing more
than not to make a spectacle
but my mother insists he fill it with stones.

The stone father is anchored
to the armchair, while the other
goes upstairs to his room in a sulk.

The stone father holds the television control,
orchestrates the night's entertainment.
The other stays asleep like a bear.

Helen Ivory

What the House Said

When the sky feeds me birds,
I cough them up
in the middle of your parlour games.

When you examine them
you'll see even the most vivid
burnt crow-black.

I do not have to pretend to like you,
we have signed no contract
yet you line my insides with your lives.

Hollie McNish

My Boyfriend Can Cook

I'm sitting, slightly tipsy sipping from a bottle of white wine
taking my time
watching my man like a fine dine
Aphrodite, the mighty god, blessed me
he's cooking for me
it's wet and messy
he's peeling the sauté potatoes, I'm tasting spicy aromas
smelling like cravings
bathing naked in the scent from the cooker

I look at him.
He smells sweet like a pod of vanilla.

Rosemary buds, hot pepper, thyme and steam
a little sweat drips from his brow and it's time to dream
I imagine screaming naked in a field of strawberries
drowning in custard and cream, I'm getting sore please
he wipes his face, a little glance my way
sipping on his liquor, my lips ready to play
stray sizzling colours mix with sensual smells
my body sweat mingles waiting for that tingle from the timers bell
I want to yell, but I sit there caressed, eying up
steaming pans on hobs like clouds of sweet breath
he's just making dinner, I'm making babies in my head
he passes me asparagus tips soft dressed in lemon
tickling my tongue as I suck them
then I'm licking on the starter melon
sweet juice from the fruit running down my chin
a little giggle, juice trickles down my nipples and g string
the potatoes are boiling
oil heating like a piece of warm skin
I imagine my body so oily boiling on top of him

it's nearly time

as red wine like deep sighs he pours into the sauce
I'm getting wet just waiting for his main course
hard wooden spoon he holds stirring that gravy
circular motion, soft, firm, like when he makes me come
adds a bit of rum, a pinch of pepper and salt
candles flicker, knickers wet as he takes the pot.

Now I'm standing by the cooker in a loose dress
his hand dips in the sauce and I taste it off his
slow motion, my warm lips wrapped round his finger
slow pulling and as the fresh flavours linger in my mouth
my tongue tastes the rest of
broccoli and green beans
cream sauce and sweetness
dripping taste from my thighs to my chest.

My plate is licked clean.
My tastebuds hurt.
I lie back.
Already ready for dessert.

Hollie McNish

Signs

No one grows here any more, No one calls this place a home
Cos only houses line this town and signs that show you where to go
No welcome signs, no signs of life, at night the signs all cut like knives
No entry to no underage. No music bars, no clubs, no raves
No under 18 no ID. No where to dance no where to be
Like ghosts the youth now shuffle round. Youth clubs closed, walkmans drowned
At night no under 21s inside. By day no play no ball games signs
No throwing catch, no football sparks, no kicks no goals save broken glass
No skateboarding no skates no crowns. Keep off the grass,
Keep off. Keep out
In parks the signs all switch the same
All over 14s stay away
No roundabouts, no swings, no slides, no growth no games no welcome signs
So, now Boredom.
It stinks of shit
from sewers seeps to streets to poison kids, preaching, it lies in gutters lined
with broken kicks, deflated footballs, grime and teenage sick
in lines of coke and late night shifts it sniffs each day in painful habits, breeding
like rabbits, vermin hatched, finding fun in grabbing handbags
like a hammock, sagging centres, minds left numb and stomachs emptied, it
snatches fire-filled beating hearts, pouring water over sunken sparks, through
stolen dreams and dawning lights, waits outside pubs for pointless fights, turns
kids to hate and adults reeling, minds to crime and hands to stealing, with
nothing left nothing to do, turning towns to human zoos, caged and locked in
pathways blocked, think of only cock or watching clocks, as young people wait
and rot, labelled yobs by headline cops, nowhere to go, no breaths are baited,
youth clubs closed and playgrounds gated, boredom reigns on teenage crownsm
ghostly village, cities, towns, as others frown and walk away, looking down on
youth today
As children play now let us pray
Boredom will not spoil their way.

Irvine Welsh

The Twa Rides

Divorced and lonely Christmas Eve
Ma heid a riot ay plans n peeve
At Princes Street oan that fine day
Ah spied twa rides come by ma way

Each ride had great big muckle tits
Tae thrill a country lad tae bits
The lassies looked sae fine n gleesome
Ah stoaped thaime tae suggest a threesome

Ah said tae yin (the biggest ride)
'Come tae yon flat whaire ah do bide.
Ah'll plough yir mucky field aw day.'
(It's standard chat doon Ayrshire way.)

While ah wis pished but far fae cunted
Yon city rides were black affronted
As yin lass slapped ma bonny face
The other shot ma een wi mace

Ah fell in tears tae hard asphalt
They carried oan their grim assault
Ah felt stiletto heel pierce baw
And Edinburgh polis they did ca'

So up afore yon magistrate
Ah must confess he wisnae great:
'No fair maiden of oor Edina
Wants an Ayrshire hound at her vagina!'

'A West Coast blackguard' he did craw
Ah couldnae even say: 'yir maw!'
At Saughton Beast's wing ah'd reside
Tae wear that maroon shirt wi pride

They pit ays in a narray cell
Wi six fit fower ay strappin hell
An organ that wid cleave yir erse
Till ye left yon prison in a hearse

'Listen guid, ma Ayrshire laddie
Oan the beasts wing ah'm the daddy
And in here ah've ma ain wee law
The rides, they nivir stoap at twa!'

Jenni Fagan

Poem after Listening to Neruda

What we want, it so happens, we are.

I am sick,
a waterproof swan staring into the wombs of horses,
I am the still wool,
I am the elevator's spectacles.

You—are how nature is separated,
and it so happens I am sick, and you are fingernails, hair and shadow.

A giant hand—so marvellous.
On the stair, where he killed a man with a balloon in his ear, my green knife.

A stretched-out sleep,
my
breathing.

Everyday,
a wounded wheel.

Television
reflected
in my windows. Hideous.

Come on chicken, hang over the houses I hate, be a coffee pot!

Venom is umbilical,
bye bye grandma—under the house,
buzzing gas again.

Send out a kite, a kite to catch,
it will fly by your window, go on—look out now, it won't destroy you.

Forget everything.

The park-light (is gold) and the people are beginning to point,
the sky—is opening.
Look out now, it won't destroy you.

Jenni Fagan

He Groped Me on the Dance Floor;
I Should Have Knocked Him Out

He claimed he was a fetishist,
(liar)
he had a penchant for anal
(receiver)
he was hopeful,
for more kink than corn.

I made an eight with my waist,
(bent) to sweep
the long-grass aside,
bent to (hear)
moon-time crickets
chit-chit-chat.

He asked if I had (known)
many Frankensteins…
or frogs?
Being as I was
the (corsets) bones,
inelegant smoker
of souls.

Jenni Fagan

The Sun Made Me Strong

The sun made me strong,
it told the moon
I wouldn't wear shoes
or return calls
or be much of anything,
the sun
told the moon
I was only ever going to be a bit of fluff
at the back of the sofa,
or just some pale rumour
no one listened to,
just dust
from bricks that block windows,
just a reflection
in a kettle
that fades when it gets cleaned.

Jenni Fagan

Cold as a Girl

Icicles
like
narwhal
tusks,
or the gnarled
bony
finger
of winter
herself.

JL Williams

Zobop Ska's Not Dead Weird Glow

I've
played in
bands since school
and I was a
a terrible musician
Eight miles high It's not
like a real conscious decision
for me male strippers Music makes
hard edges disappear I've played in
bands since eight miles high you can't always
get what you want unknown pleasures Male
strippers There's different versions eight
miles high Gold silver white
black monochromatic
You're tracing the edge
of the room unknown
pleasures It
becomes
a
kinda
group exercise
Money man parish
eight miles high it's
not like a real conscious
decision for me How do
I fill a space and empty you
can't always you're tracing the edge of
the room male strippers Unknown pleasures
Selecting the colour the
width of the colour it
becomes a kinda
money man parish
there's different
versions
music

makes hard
edges disappear
gold silver male
strippers The colour
range for that is nine different
colours, sometimes seven money
man parish I didn't actually
need to be there all the time making
it eight miles high essentially
I don't money man parish eight unknown
pleasures gold silver white black
monochromatic essentially
I don't need to be
there money man
I didn't
actually
need
to be
there all unknown
there's different versions
the colour range for
male strippers music makes
selecting the colour the
width of the colour you're tracing
the male strippers it becomes a kinda
group exercise there's You can't always get
what you want how do I fill a space
and empty a space at the same
time Essentially I don't
need to be there

*The words used in this poem are drawn from an
interview with the Glaswegian artist Jim Lambie.
It was first read at* Neu! Reekie! *at Jim's Poetry Club.*

Jock Scot

Above The Volcano

We climbed to the top of Arthur's Seat
And looked down on the castle
Through the haar you could see Inchkeith
And in the city, the glint of granite
Was caught in the setting sun
At that moment when we two were one
Standing there together
With the whole town spread before us
The sun set over Glasgow way—and, yes!
The colours they were glorious.

Then the lights came on
And street by street
A transformation transformed
Leith Walk, George Street, Easter Road,
With Clermiston beyond.

I was trying to explain to you how I felt
I was going on and on
But you weren't even listening—
You were humming a Bob Dylan song.

We were slipping on the shallow earth
Where the rock broke through;
The rock was breaking through
The shallow earth.
You slipped, and I caught you, and you laughed,
Just then.
As I prayed that the moment would never end.

The end.

Jock Scot

3 Furies

I met you—*just*—when I stepped off the straight and narrow,
But luckily I fell into your arms
Happy! to give up the pointless struggle
I willingly surrendered to your charms
You could see I was unhappy, you
could see I was insane,
You loved me like a healer
Not just once, but again and again
A cloud burst in the sky as I asked you why?
What I needed was a hankie, but all you gave me
Was a tissue of lies
Your beautiful smile concealed underneath
The horrible fact that you were lying through your teeth
But all the Happy Days did not prepare me (oh no)
For the day you led me up the garden path.
Lookin' back I should've seen it comin',
I remember that you had to look away
As you coldly blurted out my curt dismissal
I replied, 'Is that all you've got to say?'
Now you don't seem to have a good word for me
I spend my days just smokin', and sittin', and
doin' my knittin'.
Waitin' round for the postman to deliver letters
That you haven't even written.
I'm reduced to sitting round for sixteen hours
In the vain hope that maybe you will call
What a massive disappointment
Just another girl after all

Additional verse/optional

The day you broke my heart
I also broke my wrist
I tried to chin you outside the pub
But, you ducked and I missed.

Kapka Kassabova

It's Always Strange to Sleep in Cities

For Marti Friedlander

It's always strange to sleep in cities
you haven't seen in daylight.
You could be anywhere, anyone
could breathe next door while
under used blankets you dream
of waking to the world's highest spires,
fastest clouds, brightest snow.

You dream of drunken rooftops
strewn with shards of broken stars
and you dream of the people you loved.
And suddenly, they're down in the streets,
in this city of shadows and light.
It seems they've always been here.

And you tell them without words
because words are not
in the nature of this dream
how much has happened since.
How strange you find it to be here.
How hurt is the future, the past too.

They thank you for your visit,
everything is fine, they say,
their mouths opening without a voice,
their manner growing distant and suspicious,
everything is fine. Then dawn
breaks over the city, and they are gone.

Kapka Kassabova

Berlin—Mitte*

I live in a haunted house.
I have lost my hunger. I have lost my sleep.
When I sleep, my dreams are not mine.

My sense of time is unstable
and I wait for anonymous
midnight visits. I feel that all
that is to come is inevitable.

I have my suitcase close-by, but it's empty—
I know I'll be surprised. I'm ready
to leave my possessions behind.

I look for clues around the house.
But the walls are whitewashed.
The ceilings are too high.
The floor has been treated with the polish
of this new, confident century.

I fear they will come one night,
after sixty years of absence.
I will offer them the house of course, the bed,
the kitchen table, but I fear they will say
that what was taken from them
can never be given back.

*Mitte is traditionally the Jewish
neighbourhood of Berlin.*

Kevin Williamson

Pauli's Exclusion Principle

When the front door is bolted shut
it is according
to the laws of quantum physics.
None shall pass.

Subtract man from woman
porno on a loop
sativa gold
& sweet black coffee.

Pauli's Exclusion Principle
describes it
with scientific accuracy as:
My Own Private Amsterdam.

In such laboratory conditions
poetry can be created
whose density exceeds that
of the smoke.

The process is contradictory
self-explanatory
black but not bleak
allows no room for error.

Dub
the final piece of the jigsaw.
Rhythm of a cough.
Notes from underground.

Kevin Williamson

Take Your Pick

Haggerston Castle or Blackpool Pier?
Ingmar Bergman or Lars von Trier?

Janey Jones or Patti Smith?
Rock Hudson or Montgomery Clift?

Purple Haze or Lambert & Butler?
Pam Ayres or Ivor Cutler?

Casino Royale or You Only Live Twice?
Bill Douglas or Bill Forsyth?

Haggis Burrito or Irn Bru Sorbet?
Pat Stanton or Franck Sauzee?

Myra Hindley or Rosemary West?
Diego Maradona or Georgie Best?

Elio Petri or Antonioni?
Kurt Cobain or Lena Zavaroni?

John Lydon or Joe Strummer?
Chaka Khan or Donna Summer?

Jinglin Geordies or Ensign Ewart?
Ayrton Senna or Jackie Stewart?

The House of Commons or Fingal's Cave?
Rule Britannia or Scotland The Brave?

Margaret Thatcher or Edward Heath?
Screamadelica or Sunshine on Leith?

Tunnocks Teacakes or Custard Creams?
Sun Ra or Tangerine Dream?

Hannibal Lecter or Raskolnikov?
John Wayne Bobbit or Vincent van Gogh?

Willie MacRae or Hilda Murrell?
Jelly Beef Whiskas or Taco Bell?

Lee Scratch Perry or Martin Hannett?
Davie Cooper or Eammon Bannon?

Tam Paton or Simon Cowell?
Whitman's Song or Ginsberg's Howl

The Ayatollahs or The Septic Tanks?
Ronnie Simpson or Gordon Banks?

Sleeping Beauty or the Blarney Stone?
Jack The Ripper or Bible John?

Grizzly Man or Gorillas in the Mist?
The Bitter End or a Lemon Twist?

Muriel Spark or Margaret Drabble?
Leon Brittan or Jimmy Savile?

Kirsty Logan

Sacred Heart Basement, Del Rio, 1997

1.
it's because of the boys my momma says
and she sure would know because she's had more than anyone.

lined up along the fence they were
noon till dusk, hats in their hands and shoes scuffing the dirt.

that's what everyone says
and everyone knows everyone here. and I sure know lots of boys.

momma says church camp
is for girls to make good but there are enough boys to share.

a different one every day
behind the kitchen annexe, breath sticky and dicks hard as marbles.

2.
sacred heart basement smells
of stewed broccoli and boysweat and aircon and drugstore bodyspray.

pastor says welcome and forgive
then it's on to praising and stomping, singing and fainting.

just in time for damnation.
it's the girls, says the pastor, *snake-charmers, hypnotists, bellies of sin*

you keep away, he says
and I wonder just how I'm supposed to keep away from myself.

the end is coming, he says
repent repent before it's too late REPENT SINNERS AND SERPENTS.

the sky rumbles in a threat
of thunder, and then it's not the sky but the world, the world and us

the walls the floor the roof
shake shudder howl rearrange and we're screaming we're crying the world is
ending and so are we and I repent oh lord I repent I'm sorry I am a sinner I am
a serpent but I repent I respond I repose I am yours I'll never I'll never again

3.
at school I find out that a parent
suggested that the end of the world would purge our sins.

the church camp counsellors dropped tables
on the floor of the dining room over the basement.

two weeks after the end of the world
I go behind the school cafeteria with the new boy.

I know whose parent
gets the danger of sin. *it's because of your momma* the boys said.

Kirsty Logan

sunday morning lie-in

i'm staying down here
until i make her sing
louder than church

Krystelle Bamford

For My Nephew, Age Two

Apple Baby, here you are
with your lily-bellied roar:
A! B! C! D! Filaments
incandescent even
in the soil—the glimmer
of some forked and shaded thing.

I was there when you first
staggered straight across the kitchen.
Oh my god, the pride on your face—
the prince of this world and all
of us, subjects. Then the fall,
of course, into our sprung arms.

These steps towards
some other place outside
all this, our squatting, beaming
selves—not hubristic
or ill-judged, just
the way forward.

And us, fated to become
patient, dusty demigods
seen mostly at Christmas.
But listen, AB—the mutter
of our beads, the beginning,
now, and always: X Y Z.

Krystelle Bamford

Covenant

If I was a covenant of grace,
my sister was a covenant of works.
If she was made in China, I
was spun at the hearth.
When she coughs, clouds gather,
then purple, then rain.
When I move, Sweet William
spells me in three separate colors.
If I am light on fresh straw,
she is the rat taking shelter
from the squall. But then
her province lies elsewhere:
the thick, rolling smell
of rain's onset, the grace
of unexpected dark,
the eyes of the one
who made her
among millions,
the mixed mercy
of the long drop.

Lach

7.10.10

In smallest styles the universe winks
A giggle at a funeral
A step that isn't there

In a meadow by the roadside
sweating from changing a flat
a car slowed to ask if I was alright
and then
I was

Liz Lochhead

Connecting Cultures

I am talking in our lingua franca.
Tell me, do you drive on the left or right?
Is your football team the *Botswana Zebras*
Or *Indomitable Lions of Cameroon*?
Can you take me to *Junkanoo*
And is there mangrove forest?
Is it true that a lightweight business suit
Is the appropriate city-garb and shaking hands
The usual form of greeting?
Are there frigate birds? Diamonds? Uranium?
What is the climate? Is there a typical hurricane season
Or a *wind of change*?
How many miles of coastline in your country?
Is the currency the Kenyan shilling or the
Brunei dollar—or is it also the word for *rain* or *a blessing*?
Do you speak the lingua franca?

Communication can mean *correspondence*,
Or *a connecting passage or channel*, can mean
A means of imparting and receiving information such as
Speech, digital media, Facebook, the press and cinema.
Communications can mean *means of transporting, especially*
Troops or supplies.

Commonwealth means
A free association of independent member nations bound by
Friendship, loyalty, the desire for
Democracy, equality, freedom and peace.
Remembering how hard fellow feeling is to summon
When Wealth is what we do not have in Common,
May every individual
And all the peoples in each nation
Work and hope and
Strive for true communication—
Only by a shift and sharing is there any chance

For the Welfare of all our people and Good Governance.
Such words can sound like flagged-up slogans, true.
What we merely say says nothing—
All that matters is what we do.

Liz Lochhead

Nina's Song

Nina, come to Scotland
Nina come soon
We'll show you the wee-est field-mouse
And the biggest, roundest moon.

The million-zillion stars'll *amaze* you—
So bright and so far…
—Pick one and we'll sing you

Twinkle, twinkle little star

Come soon, Nina,
Come and never wonder why
There can be three perfect rainbows
In just one wide sky—

Just enjoy the bonny colours—
Nina, never mind their names—
Although—it's true—
We will very much enjoy teaching you
Your *red, orange, yellow, green and blue*
Your *violet and indigo*—
Your *red, orange, yellow, green and blue*
Wee Nina, all the same.

And Glenuig will be glad to see you
All the singing birds will go:
Nice to meet you, new wee Nina
Hey Nina—hello!

McGuire

The Glasgae Boys

Glasgay gender bending sex offending
all soft down The Merchant of Penis,
down Glasholegreen,
down The Gallowgay,
down SuckyMaHoleStreet,
down Tendergrove Park,
down the WestBenders.

Q: What do you get if you mix Green with Blue?
Answer: Turquoise.
Q: What do you get if you mix White and Red?
Answer: Pink.

O, the pink and turquoise boys.
Come roll yir bawz around way each other.
The boys in the pink and turquoise,
ma Son better not play for the other side.

Aggression in The Bar for Repressed
Homo-Erotic memories.
Knife Crime as metaphorical sodomy.

Affection is a laughing matter,
all feeling reduced to a wank
after a few pints over some blonde number
with her hair bleached right to the cerebral cortex.

Fitbawmen way daffodil hearts
drinking under the table their tender selves, a
soaking in the pub, splashing in the shallows,
seeking carnal pleasure down the Clyde.

Gender bending sex offending.
Get that boy down the boxing ring,
we'll make a punch bag out of him yet!

(But have you seen his calf muscles?
Smooth as marble long caramel brown,
tight as a taut rope.)

Poofs, man, who needs them?
—Bennets Shite Club
—Polo Nob jockeys
—The Glasgow Pink Pound.
O chasing after the pink pound
with a feather out stretched to tickle an arsehole.

My son could have danced
Billy Elliot down in London
but he hung himself from a penis
and tied his mother around his neck.
Rather he swung from a tree
than fir the other side.

Glasgow used to be a knife.
Glasgow used to be a gangland Disneyland.
Glasgow used to be an old man's pub.
Glasgow used to be a betting man's game.
Glasgow used to be the razor against the soft cheek.
Glasgow used to have a third world life span.
Glasgow used to belt her pupils red raw.
Glasgow used to drink her men to the graveyard.
Glasgow was all Woodbine, bitter and bookies.
(Naw pal, that was just a Peter Mullan film.)
Glasgow is all cappuccinos and croissants.
Glasgow is all baguettes and pains au chocolat.

Just ask Billy Connolly. His father molested him.
Poor Billy, aye. Wouldn't be half the man he was today
if he wasn't first robbed of half the child he could have been.

Glasgow—whit's yir agender?
Hetero-normative default setting,

none of this metro-sexual, rainbow
on the horizon, bisexual reality,
ying and yang,

woman inside of the man
inside of the woman
inside of the man.
None of this hetero-flexible, omni-sexual,
bending a little, frying pan sexuality.
I'm a man's man but not a man's man for *'aw that'*.

Glasgow. We not tend to it,
but watch it blacken like a burst eye,
blacken like a coal pit,
blacken like a dead flower.
We do not tend to feeling.
Centuries of shame, shadowing the city.

Michael Pedersen

Gravity

I love you
she said, as if wearing someone
else's skin,
as if clocking-in
then out
of the nine to five
that tired her bones.
I love you she said
with the forced verve of waves
gargling oily pebbles from
a spill, its fringe a congealing shoreline; talk
laced with salt; a tongue
socked in sand. *I love you*
she said, with the mechanical bareness
of a warden clamping a car to the pavement,
the payment meter and itself;
choking on diesel that once
made an engine purr; a majestic gull sifting
through a city's birthing gunk, cum,
love's tragic overspill.
I love
she said
I love
you
with the frankness of caffeinated truths
in the morning after our own golden Armageddon
which is as welcome as Nirvana.
I love you, half price,
with the candour of when we never really knew each other;
bridal curiosity ringing, rings setting up the eyes.
I love you
in the way
we never touch upon in joviality;
in a way
we never rediscovered that raw sexuality;

in the way we
have time to tread
water—that's no good thing.

I love you with saccharine warmth
for our own self-pleasantries,
with everything we're floating;
we promised to make things float;
were we not supposed to
(this once made us) F L O A T?

Michael Pedersen

Highland Koo

you are massive
and ginger, no effulgent like Irn-Bru
but light and sandy, pollens and rust.

King o' Celts, lionised as thistles and
oor Rabbie—yer puss ower postcards,
tea towels and rubbishy tins.

You'd dae fine in London or America,
alien of extraordinary ability, but
those hooves wouldnae

trot anywhere else. Koo yer horns
are like Triassic tusks atop yer heid,
reckon you could square-go a tiger

if bullied along, put Desperate Dan
on his erse—nae bother; but you're no bam
Koo, naw, starting nuthin with naeone,

fringe over yer een, bonfire in thon
belly, sure, you play it cool, scoff
grass, scart yerself rotten on fences,

power through the shitey weather
take a plunge in the modest sun
drink it in, as yiv a'ways done.

Miriam Gamble

Pledge

After Alistair MacLeod

Made to travel on her own
she will trash the box, utter a cold sweat.
For her, knowledge is merely hope,
her head over the door.

A swallow travels on her back
in the summer, scissoring your path
as you stride down off the hill.
Horse heeds the hand she trusts,
will follow anywhere.

Horse foaled before you had her,
knows what it is to child-bear,
though horses will drive their own young off,
after a time, mares as well as males.

The home of horse resides in you:
you love her more, even,
than you might love a child,
her own love being blinder.
You arked this flood together.
Horse must never be betrayed.

Miriam Gamble

Reflexology

The plug on the hoover is greasy
after the flooding from the upstairs flat;
you think briefly
as you insert it into the wall,
then flick the switch and start to clean.

You wonder afterwards at your choice
which must have been one,
though you don't remember making it.
There is not even a terrorist,
this time, for you to say you won't be cowed

though you blame it anyway on where you're from: you say
into your own salty palm
that you learned to live like this.
Even your palm knows the argument is crude.
Its little patch of eczema stares you down.

Paul Reekie

One Day of Lions

(1)

In a little room at James Thins
We're photographed by Harpers and Queens
Everyone fairly dressed up
Janet and Irvine and Anne
Rosie, Sean Connery and Stan
Me in a tartan tie—as befits an
Occasion such as this
We're guests but we don't fit in with
The assembled great and good
Wine dished out by nice waiters
Elevenses—I get my snout in the trough
Awards for those bound in paper and cloth
(It's a half rhyme, but that's—fine)
A nice meal at the music college in the Cowgate
Picking chicken amongst the ancient instruments
Crawford says he's seen Williamson
and Burn do a poem with backing music on the TV
I say what of it
I say and what of it

(2)

He says I just wonder if it would work on the page
I say it sits on the page, it stands
On the page. It does fuckin aerobics
On the page

Cairns of the Arts Council comes over
To talk to Irvine. So I hear you're
Leaving us for Holland...
I go out for a smoke and here's
McCabe. I give him some chat of
The trade. He says he doesn't know

Where to put poems nowadays.
I say well never mind that look at
This: A little sheet of blotters with a
Celtic design. He hasn't seen LSD
For a long time. He's got to pick up
The kid this after; I understand. He asks
About my girlfriend but I don't
Ask about his.

Our party peel off from the litterati
Acid and speed kicking in. We
Decide to go to the pictures. We see
One and a half weddings and no
Funerals.
The sun comes out as we
Hit South Clerk St

{Silver Maxims}

She said, 'I never liked David Adamson since he spread it round the school that
he fingered me in the phone box.'

(4)

One Day of Lions

Browning: Ripostes.   Schadenfreude
                             Malicious joy (lit.)
                             or joy in others' misfortune (gossip)

More B/way bollocks: Petrushka's west of Broadway (48th St) Dance to a bala-
laika orchestra - Six chorus girls to the tune of 'Goodnight Sweetheart'. Swell
black and white spaldings
Movie for 75 in the Globe. Hunt Club 123 West Fortyfifth St a 'speak' with
18,000 members. Hollywood Restaurant 'nakedest floorshow ever seen'
Front orchestra box at the palace Burns and Allen. 1932, Minsky's Republic

'Decent music, indecent chorus, swell strippers, figures displayed, suggestive and filthy.'
Next door to see 'Palmy Days' Honeymoon Lane. 50th St and B/way. 'Kitty' Get Phillip's magnesia toothpaste. Starlight roof of the Waldorf.

—

It's flip time.

Paul Reekie

Untitled

(1)

In lieu forever of scholarly work:
Coleridge in Edinburgh 1803
there he lay in the Black Bull
at length
and close to screaming
there lay Coleridge writing
'The Pains of Sleep'
Poor Coley who died as he lived
a-dreaming
Shot dead while sleeping
by the gout within
Alone and all unknown
at Edinburgh in an inn
[too close to the bone man]
Neither poppy nor mandragoria
nor smack made Kubla Khan.
A teacher tells me over a
sniffter in the staff room:

(2)

Aye clubs and drugs, clubs and
drugs that's all they care
about the young ins.

Say
'Nae shit!'

———————————

Opium, laudanum
Coleridge, de Quincy. De Quincy—
A real-life Greyfriar's Bobby

at the hands of Edinburgh landlords.
Coleridge on the horrors of
insomnia: (pause) Opium would not
give me sleep.
What it did give me was . . .
uh repose.

(3)

I take a class.
Kid says to me like this:
You're giving us this Koobly Khan poem
and this Coleridge
What's this to do with nowadays?
What's Koobly Khan and Trainspotting
got in common?
Oh.
Say like: Opium derivatives,
The fact that
drugs induce reveries that aren't
imagination.
Edinburgh
and oh—harmonious diction.

Ron Butlin

While walking on Salisbury Crags, James Hutton [1726–97] came across rock formations that seemed to contradict Bishop Ussher's accepted chronology of the world's creation in 4,004 BC. Hutton, 'the Father of Geology', published his findings during the years when the French Revolution was at its bloodiest.

James Hutton Learns to Read
the Hieroglyphics of the Earth

Woken once too often by the *rattle-clatter*
of tumbril wheels on cobbles, the *click…click…*
click of distant knitting needles,
James Hutton decided never to go
to sleep again.

Then, by the light of several Edinburgh Council moons
(spares, in case the heavens were taken over
by the church), he tip-toed past storm-wrecked
Holyrood Abbey, went striding down
unimagined corridors,
through undreamt-of walls and doors where
Scottish Hope would one day
be cemented into place
(the bars across its parliament windows
wooden, just in case).

The Park…The Salisbury Crags…

where several hundred million years ago the Earth
cracked itself wide open—

                    *

Detailed as a map of Man's undiscovered self,
zigzag Time lies flat-packed,
for everyone to see…

Stacked magma, olivine, dolerite chilled to glass,
eternity crushed to lines of slowly
spelled-out hieroglyphics, and cut
in blood-red haematite.

...and Hutton *sees* it. He's the first!

First to know he walks upon an ancient ocean floor
(God's Flood, the merest puddle in all *that* vastness).
First to hear the stone-hard heartbeat *pound-pound-*
pounding out Existence.

Elsewhere, Revolution has taken to the streets
with an accusation and a scream,
a guillotine-swish...
French clocks run backwards to Year One.

Sunday 23rd October 4,004 BC?
All in the blink of a biblical eye! says Hutton.

*

Meanwhile, you and I continue turning
on our axis to the *tick*...
tick...tick of Time that never
started *Once upon a* ...
And will surely never, ever—

Ah, these strata, these infinities glimpsed between!

Ron Butlin

While on convalescence at Craiglockart Hospital from wounds sustained at the Western Front, Wilfred Owen [1893–1918] decided to return to his company. He was killed a week before the Armistice.

Wilfred Owen Reads between the Lines

Advance two steps/back two steps…
Breathless mouths get stopped with mud.
Advance two steps/back two steps…

Our generation's on the terrace sitting the next dance out,
chairs lined up to catch the sun.
Below, a goods train trundles its clank of wagons
west into the future . . . Then it's gone.
Edinburgh's mapped out at our feet—its chimney smoke,
the Castle, Calton Hill, the Forth, the coast of Belgium,
the distant fields of France . . .

The impossibly young nurse who heals each wounded day
now takes my hand in hers. Turns it over.
'These lines,' she tells me, 'will show . . .'
And how lightly she traces out the track of an approaching bullet.
The smog-yellow drift of gas.
A mortar shell's sudden thud full-stop.

I can already hear the barbed-wire laughter stripping us
of flesh and bone as, one by one,
we clamber up to heaven, a company of angels soaring
into the ever-blue—

This is a dance we cannot live through.

Ron Butlin

Transport initiatives are currently all the rage in Edinburgh, in every sense of the word. In an effort to calm the civic breast, here is a modest suggestion.

The Gondolas of South Bridge

Trapped by a Scottish downpour that's already lasted centuries,
we're outside Poundstretcher's, stuck in the bus shelter.
Here the heavens can fall only so far, pooling
into the shallow metal lake inches above our head.
We wait, and dream of gondolas.

—*Some rain, eh?* says one man, gazing upstream to Surgeon's Hall
and downstream to the Tron.
—*Call this rain?* Says another, gobbing into the flood
(he's ankle-deep and loving it).
*The cistern that was flushed empty long, long ago
is only now starting to refill. Soon the Castle'll have a moat,
tides'll break upon the shores of Princes Street.*

—*These gondolas?* A woman asks.
—*Aye? A new transport initiative? An integrated system with the buses, so that—?*
—*Ye've seen yer last bus.*
—*With the trams then, so that—?*
—*Trams!* (another gob mightier than the last) *Gon-dol-as, I'm telling you!
Our only hope in this damn climate. Fleets of them,
flotillas, convoys lining up along the City Bypass.
We'll hear them serenading nearer when the time comes.*

Meanwhile our city drowns—an underwater gridlock of good intentions stalled,
rusting to a standstill.

Like it or not, we were all born yesterday.
Who can tell what this deluge means to the clans of Scottish fish
patrolling their puddled wee lochan above?
Theirs is a soundless ceilidh.

When the waters rise enough to flood them out, will they glide off
with a tartan flick of the tail to swim the Gardens,
the New Town, Leith and out to sea?

Leaving us to develop gills ourselves?

Sandra Alland

Flip

So after her place, I
emptied the recycling, brushed
my teeth, thought of England
in the way only a Scot can.
Then sleep and I sank into each other.

Loving her in my dream was easier,
unless you count the tentacles. But her
face lacked that pinched thing, her accent wasn't
so posh. When she spread her many legs,
she said, 'Love is the cure for colonialism!'
I laughed heartily, knowing
love had failed at ambitions far less lofty.
Before I woke up, she whispered, 'Auld lang syne.'

Sandra Alland

Tilt

'Better off banging your head on that
lamppost than wishing an
injection of humanity into some ugly
sodding fascist.'
She yelled this over a pint of ale,
ferociously fiddling with her
unkempt hair, licking those
lovely anarchist lips.

Times like that I lack all poetry.
I stutter and blush, feel
my body go lascivious, my brain
exit stage left. Some politics are that
sexy. 'Hmmm,' I said, tongue buzzing.

Scott Hutchison

Silence, North Carolina

Aye, silence. Aside
from the creak of the world as it turns,
aside from the hustle of the wild
and the snap of time
clicking into place again
and again; aside from the boot
of the ground, miles away
probably. Aye, silence
'round here. Aside
from the sniff of the wind
or these rattling lungs
or cigarette fizz
or the putt of a fox foot
as its red roam begins.
Aside from the clatter of homes and the start of a car,
from the purr of stones beneath arriving tyres.
Aye. Silence round here.
Aside from these riotous words through
your dizzy old skull: *do something
to break this, you can have it
again.* There's never just silence
when you're not here.

Tim Wells

Is it True What They Say about the Posh Kids at Uni?

That it's full of 'em?
Drugging, drinking,
humping, pumping,
protesting and feathering
the nesting?
I heard one girl,
so public school
she's an anarchist,
blew a bloke
at the Slavoj Zizak
afterparty.
Right there!
She didn't care.
But don't fret,
In a couple of years
she'll be in the meeja,
an estate agent,
a banker.
Then we'll all get fucked.

Tim Wells

The Daily Grind

It's not that I'm sipping coffee
where once costermongers
swigged mugs of tea—
things change, we know that,
hope for it even—
but that the dreams they had
and I strive for still,
that they amount to nothing, as do we.

That never changes.
The more the tamping,
the more bitter the brew.
What really bites the cupcake
is that even the little we have,
the bastards feel entitled to that too.

Tim Wells

There but for the Grace of Bauhaus

The beige vomit
trailed down her front
sits vivid
against the black
of her coat.
Nightbuses
are indeed
a fantasy world.
The spatters
on her faux fur collar
smize.
Though she is fierce,
unrepentant
and glorious,
in her drunkenness
the puke in her hair
makes it difficult
to commit.
The stranger
sat next to me
must think the same.
For she smiles
and we both laugh.
I stand for my stop
and she whispers
'get home safe.'
The goth
heaves into a newspaper.
David Cameron's face
looks appalled.

Tom Leonard

The Cesspit and the Sweetie Shop

Thoughts-in-progress (Feb 2014) on Westminster and the Scottish Referendum

The Cesspit

The government was run
by one who had made his
career in Public Relations,
and Public Relations was the
ever-there, the oil and glue
of what had been, and
Public Relations maintained
was still, representative
parliamentary democracy.
But representative of what,
and whom, and which?

Of Public Relations itself
it seemed, a not-quite empty
set of had-to-be recorded
signs and actions, running
parallel but contrary to what
people knew and experienced.
A ritual: the acquired signs
of meaning and personal
sincerity outwardly shown
by rote: a ritualisation of the
concept of democracy and
dialogue, masquerading as
dialogue and democracy itself.

People outside the lateral
inter-relationship of Press
and politics felt somehow
the world they knew had

nothing to do with the world
they saw and heard reported.
Endless the flip-chart mentality
about nought point five or was it
eight of 'growth'; 'experts'
from thinktanks were the norm,
never the ordinary daily rising
cost of food seen in the shops,
the gas, the electric bills long
since gone crazily upward.

Historic societal conflict
was redefined, no longer
rich versus poor, worker
against employer, capital
versus labour. The culture
and its language had been
systematically changed.
Granted, historic injustices
of men over women, white
over black, straight over
gay were taken up and
countermanded in part
by law; but never in such
a way as to question the
new ubiquitious orthodoxy,
the daily myth proposed
of central societal struggle:
'the taxpayer' versus the
drain on the taxpayer's tax.

The Sweetie Shop

A clear majority won
its first rebranding was
the name 'government'
itself; decreed and taken up
forthwith by public media
as if the undisputed
and indisputably apposite
title for what had been
till then not government
at all but simply 'executive'
with ten per cent of power.
For selfstyled government,
the question now
became, as time went by
—How come our government
has only ten per cent?
Not nationalisation was
the answer, but a corporate
nationalism, whose logos
over an upbeat language
of business-diploma jargon
sprinkled with mission-statement
bullet-points, pervaded the
public bumf and websites
of this now-government's
areas of funded operation.
A sleekit mantra of jaunty
national pride became
de trop in public titles,
unnoticed largely, and
uncommented on, by
those who spread the word.

The word was 'Scotland'.
Titles across the range
of public life were binned
in root-and-branch reshaping
to present a consciousness

of stand-alone nationhood,
the nation's name declared
over and again in endstop
affirmation: *Sport Scotland,*
Education Scotland; while
'Strathclyde Police' like other
regional departments, its
headed paper, its public signs,
all that which gave it separate
identity, now was removed,
subsumed under the one
Police Scotland—albeit, creepily,
'police' be a transitive verb. What
do you do for a living, Sir Constable?
'I police Scotland,' he said.

Artists became 'creatives',
a bright and cheery term,
Creative Scotland sounded
nothing of grump or ivory tower;
amang its website bullet-points
and paths to artistic outcomes,
came news that one in four awards
would now be for work in *Scots*:
in case some glaikit southron chiel
had nay notion, links in English
were given to sites explaining
this 'national language' that
folk were supposed to scrieve in.

Across the travelling country
carriages brandished the
upbeat logo '*Scotland's Railways*';
even Jock Tamson's abused
had public institutional help renamed
Survivor Scotland. The pensioner's
bus pass no longer named a region
but bore *One Scotland* over

the national flag. Each time the pass
was daily used, the message, time
and again and again: *One Scotland*,
over the national flag.

The taboo word for card-carrying
nationalists was nationalism
itself. That word would put off
too many folk it was better to
keep onside. That which the
nationalists had been striving for
for eighty years had finally been
forced to a national crunch: and,
in a hyper-canny sleight-of-hand
worthy indeed of parliamentary
politics, it was all, in the end,
supposedly nothing to do with *them*.

For some on the Left
the Parliamentary Road
to Socialism was up
and running again.
Not since the days of
Militant in pre-New
Labour had they had
such a spring in their
step. It was a time for
leafletting and demos,
fervour at sorting out
Labour's traitors once
and for all, Get rid of
those traitorous vipers
and their one-party rule
in the West. Smash the
British State was the cry,
throw off the yoke of
Imperialism. Throw off
the yoke? Lay aside
the reins more like, the
Empire had already

thrown off its yoke, but
not with any help from
Scotland and its *bonny
fechters the warld ower.*

On the other hand
the 'no' camp
was a gallimaufray
of horrors, the
gibbering dead up
from Westminster
wrapped in the
union flag; beside
them skinheads
from the BNP,
with every hue
of far-right politic
to deepest Orange.
Rightly these said
that 1707 and the
Protestant Crown
over a single
union parliament
was chosen guarantee
of independence
from Rome over
independence from
England. Union
was itself that
guarantee. Did not
Burns himself in 1793
write that the monarch
'to speak Masonic,
is the keystone in
our royal arch
constitution'?

But Burns was
tholing his boss
for thinking him

radical; fighting
to keep his job
to feed his weans.
He was a Mason
when so was
Catholic Haydn
and Mozart of
the *Requiem Mass*
besides his great
masonic opera
The Magic Flute.

The Cesspit

Everything was done for public relations
the language-sets, their perameters
how the hands were clasped at the front
in interview, calling the interviewer by
their first name. And well they might,
they probably knew each other intimately
dined in the same clubs, flourished in the same
earnings band, each knew their job to be
management of the language environment,
an integral part of managing the economy.
Managing the economy that would
preserve their place within it as it stood.

                              Their wars were the same:
                              structural templates of PR
                              grounding a rolling
                              multi-countried occupation,
                              bombardments manned or
                              unmanned with internal
                              surveillance always allegedly
                              keeping the people safe;
                              just like the wars, just like
                              the occupations, just like
                              the bombardments manned
                              or unmanned said to be
                              'keeping the people safe'.

William Letford

The Bevy

a hid met this lassie
she liked the bevy
a like drink masel
bit this lassie liked the bevy
normally a kin keep it in check
play fitbaw n that
go oan benders
bit go a week or two withoot
regain the healthy glow
bit a hid met this lassie
an a goat a red rash beneath ma eyes
fae the bevy
drinkin too much eh it
bit a wiz enjoyin masel
cause we wid huv these brilliant arguments
proabin each other's psyche
searchin fur soft spots
seein wit damage we could dae
bit hodin back
bein cliver
niver punchin the core
cause that wiy
we could cover the soft spots wae affection
that made us feel like
we needed each other
that made us feel like
we could destroy each other
cause fawin in love wae this lassie
wiz like turnin yur chist tae the universe
an screamin hit me
bit it didnae last
cause time passed
an we realised

we couldnae hurt each other
so am back playin fitbaw n that
gon oan benders like
bit keepin it in check

William Letford

Thurs Hunnurs a Burds Oan the Roofs

here huw chouf wouf wee robin rid tit peejin breesty lovey dovey
ruffle yur feathers show me yur plume look it that Frank nut a look
nut a nut plod on then mouldy breed heed woop woop look it that
fingle foogle boogaloo that's no even a crow that's a dinosaur
thur'll be teeth in that beak that's fur sure ohh beady eye beady eye
get behind the gable she's fae the social wit a life Frank wit a life
feedin oan scraps huntin fur crumbs bit listen tae this listen tae this
we're no dodos we kin fly forget aboot the fields Frank look it the sky

Notes on Contributors

ADELLE STRIPE is a poet, editor and writer. She has released three poetry collections on Blackheath Books including the award-winning *Dark Corners of the Land*. She lives in Yorkshire and is currently a PhD student researching the life and work of the Bradford playwright Andrea Dunbar.

AIDAN MOFFAT from Falkirk has been writing and recording music since 1996, with ten years on vocals in Arab Strap, a few instrumental records as L. Pierre, an album of prose and poetry, and many collaborations. His 2011 album with Bill Wells, *Everything's Getting Older*, won the inaugural Scottish Album of the Year Award, and his first children's book, *The Lavender Blue Dress*, was published in 2014. He always wanted to move to Glasgow, so he did in 1999.

CLARE POLLARD's fourth collection of poetry, *Changeling* (Bloodaxe, 2011) is a Poetry Book Society Recommendation, and her latest book is a new translation of *Ovid's Heroines* (Bloodaxe, 2013). Her play *The Weather* debuted at the Royal Court Theatre, and her radio documentary *My Male Muse* was a Radio 4 Pick of the Year. Clare lives in South London with her husband and son, and blogs regularly about life as a poet at clarepollard.com.

DAVID KINLOCH is the author of five books of poetry including *Finger of a Frenchman* (Carcanet, 2011). His most recent publication is *Some Women* (Happenstance, 2014) which gives a voice to some famous women in the Bible. He is currently Professor of Poetry and Creative Writing at the University of Strathclyde.

DOUGLAS DUNN is a major Scottish poet, editor and critic who was the recipient of the 2013 Queen's Gold Medal for Poetry and awarded an OBE in 2003. Author of over ten collections of poetry, he has also edited several anthologies and was Professor of the School of English at the University of St Andrews from 1991 to 2008.

EMER MARTIN is a Dubliner. Her first novel *Breakfast in Babylon* was published in 1995. *More Bread or I'll Appear*, her second novel, was published internationally in 1999. She studied painting in New York and has had two solo shows of her paintings at the Origin Gallery in Dublin. Her third novel, *Baby Zero*, was published in 2007. She was awarded the Guggenheim Fellowship in 2000 and founded the publishing co-operative Rawmeash in 2014. She now lives in the swamps of Silicon Valley.

GEORGE GUNN is a poet and playwright from Caithness where he tutors at North Highland College/UHI. In 1992 he was a founder member of Grey Coast Theatre Company which toured new work around Scotland. His play *Three Thousand Trees* was a hit at the Edinburgh Festival in 2014 and his latest book of poems, *A Northerly Land,* was published by Braevalla Press in 2013 and launched at Celtic Connections. The Islands Book Trust are bringing out his prose work *The Province of the Cat* in 2015.

HELEN IVORY is a poet and assemblage artist. Her fourth Bloodaxe collection is *Waiting for Bluebeard* (2013). She edits the webzine *Ink Sweat and Tears* and teaches for the UEA/WCN online creative writing programme.

HOLLIE MᶜNISH is a UK poet who straddles the boundaries between the literary, poetic and pop scenes. She has garnered titles like 'chick of the week' (MTV) and Benjamin Zephaniah 'can't take my ears off her'. Her poetry album, *Versus,* was released in October 2014, recorded at Abbey Road Studios, London.

IRVINE WELSH is a Scottish writer currently living in the United States.

JENNI FAGAN is a Scottish poet, novelist and screenwriter who is published in nine languages; these poems are taken from her new collection—*Instruction Manual for Suicidal Girls* (boys, trolls & troglodytes). Her second novel *The Sunlight Pilgrims* is due out this year.

JL WILLIAMS' first collection, *Condition of Fire* (Shearsman, 2011), was inspired by Ovid's *Metamorphoses* and a journey to the Aeolian Islands. Her second collection, *Locust and Marlin* (Shearsman, 2014), explores the idea of home and where we come from, and was nominated for the 2014 Saltire Society Poetry Book of the Year Award. She has been published in journals including *Magma, Stand, Poetry Wales, Edinburgh Review* and *Fulcrum*. Her poetry has been translated into Dutch, Spanish, Polish, French and Greek. She plays in the band Opul and is Programme Manager at the Scottish Poetry Library.

Self-professed 'poet & tragedian', JOCK SCOT was born in Leith in 1952 and began his career in the music industry as a renowned supplier of 'good vibes'.

> 'the joc
> the dot.
> the scot
> the once teenage juice delivery boy fae the honest toun

amongst his belongings
pathological honesty &
with the perception of a ghost
lines as fast as smoke'.

—Davy Henderson on JS

KAPKA KASSABOVA is the author of the travel biographies *Street Without a Name* and *Twelve Minutes of Love*, a novel and two poetry collections. Born and raised in Bulgaria and educated in New Zealand, she now lives in the Highlands.

KEVIN WILLIAMSON is the author of one book of poetry, *In a Room Darkened* (Two Ravens Press, 2007). His babies include Rebel Inc., Bella Caledonia and Neu! Reekie!

KIRSTY LOGAN is a professional daydreamer. Her debut collection of stories is *The Rental Heart and Other Fairytales* (Salt, 2014). Her first novel, *The Gracekeepers*, was published in May 2015 in the UK, US and Canada. She lives with her girlfriend and their rescue dog in Glasgow, where she mostly reads ghost stories, listens to riot grrrl, drinks coffee, and dreams of the sea. Say hello at kirstylogan.com.

Most recently, KRYSTELLE BAMFORD's poems have appeared in *The American Poetry Review* and *The Kenyon Review*. In 2010, she was awarded a Scottish Book Trust New Writers Award and was shortlisted for the 2011 Bridport Prize. She is currently working on her first collection.

LACH is the founder of the music and art phenomenon dubbed 'Antifolk' thus insuring his historical anonymity. Lach's albums have the distinction of never being pirated. Writer/star of BBC Radio 4's comedy series *The Lach Chronicles* he's recently opted to enter the more lucrative field of poetry with the publication of *The Thin Book of Poems* (Desert Hearts Publishing). Lach spends days balancing coffee grounds into little towers. He wears his shoes inside out. A chance encounter with Freud in a café left them both bloody and aroused. He never uses his left pinky claiming it's 'God's finger'.

LIZ LOCHHEAD (born in 1947 in Newarthill, Lanarkshire) studied at the Glasgow School of Art. The first work that brought Lochhead to wider notice was *Memo for Spring*, which was published in 1972 at a time when the Scottish poetry scene was largely male-dominated. Her collections of poetry include *Dreaming Frankenstein* (1984), *True Confessions and New Clichés* (1985) and *Bagpipe Muzak* (1991). Lochhead is also a successful playwright, her productions including *Mary Queen of Scots Got her Head Chopped Off* (1987) and a Scots-language adaptation of Molière's *Tartuffe* (1985). Her latest is *Edwin Morgan's Dreams & Other Nightmares*, a play about her friend and fellow poet, Edwin Morgan. He was Scotland's first Makar, or National Poet, and when he died, she succeeded him in January 2011. Liz will be Scotland's Makar until 2016.

MᶜGUIRE is a young Scottish poet, sometimes described as a performance poet, who is pushing the boundaries of what poetry has to say with hilarious and uncompromising material about masculinity, pornography and sexuality, amongst many other subjects. McGuire has published two collections with Red Squirrel Press: *Everybody lie down and no one gets hurt* (2013) and *As I Sit Quietly, I Begin to Smell Burning* (2014). He is known for his impassioned, intense performances and can be seen regularly throughout the UK.

Edinburgh-born MICHAEL PEDERSEN has published two celebrated chapbooks, and a debut collection *Play with Me* with Polygon. He is a Canongate Future 40, a 2010 Callum McDonald Memorial Award finalist, the John Mather's Charitable Trust Rising Star of Literature 2014, as well as a budding playwright and lyricist, and the co-founder of Neu! Reekie!

MIRIAM GAMBLE is from Belfast, but now lives in Edinburgh. Her collections are *The Squirrels Are Dead* (2010), which won a Somerset Maugham Award in 2011, and *Pirate Music* (2014), both published by Bloodaxe.

PAUL REEKIE was an Edinburgh-based poet, writer and musician. He died in June 2010, aged forty-eight. Neu! Reekie! was launched in January 2011 and is named after him.

With an international reputation as a prize-winning novelist, RON BUTLIN has also been Edinburgh's Makar/Poet Laureate. He has published seven collections of poetry and given readings worldwide. He will have two new collections coming out this year: *The Magicians of Scotland* (Polygon), and verses for children, *Here Come the Trolls!*.

SANDRA ALLAND is a writer, filmmaker and interdisciplinary artist based in Edinburgh. Her most recent poetry collection, *Naturally Speaking*, won Canada's 2013 bpNichol Chapbook Award. Her poems published here previously appeared in *Blissful Times* (Toronto: BookThug, 2007). Sandra is currently co-editing a forthcoming anthology of UK disability poetics (Nine Arches Press).

SCOTT HUTCHISON is frontman for the band Frightened Rabbit, Owl John when on his lonesome, and Scott Hutchison when writing poetry.

TIM WELLS is made of lager top, Jamdown sounds, pie and mash, Toff tears and Leyton Orient FC.

Besides writing the verse reflections on it published here, TOM LEONARD spent a deal of the referendum campaign reading old Scottish parliamentary session papers together with five books on John Knox, whose 500th anniversary nobody seemed to want to talk about. Tom Leonard's most recent publication is a translation of Brecht's *Mother Courage and Her Children* in which Mother Courage speaks in the working-class language of the West of Scotland area. The volume *Definite Articles* collects his prose to 2013, *outside the narrative* gathers his poetry to 2009. Both are co-published by and available from Word Power Books in Edinburgh.

A former roofer, WILLIAM LETFORD has received a New Writers Award from the Scottish Book Trust and an Edwin Morgan Travel Bursary. His first collection *Bevel* was published by Carcanet in 2012. A chapbook of his poems *And then there was skin* was translated into Slovakian and published by Vertigo in 2014.

Note on the Type

#UntitledOne is set in New Caledonia, a digital version of
W. A. Dwiggins' classic text face Caledonia, and released by Linotype in 1982.
Poem titles are set in Avenir, designed by Adrian Fruitiger in 1988
and also released by Linotype.
The cover title and title page is set in Helvetica Neue.

The other half of *#UntitledOne* is a 21-track Neu! Reekie! double album exclusively for you, yes, YOU, the lovely purchaser of this book. Because we love you and you're special.

Your digital double album includes tracks by:

The Band of Holy Joy
Bird
Birdhead
Do The Gods Speaks Esperanto
Emelle
C.C. Sager
Jesus, Baby!
Jock Scot & Gareth Sager
Lomond Campbell
The Merrylees
Momus
Natalie Hendry
Owl John
Panda Su
Project Bona Fide
The Sexual Objects
Siobhan Wilson
Stanley Odd
TeenCanteen
Young Fathers
Wolf

To get your exclusive download code
email untitledone@birlinn.co.uk and say,
Hello! Can I get my free double album. It's that simple.

Peace & love,
Kevin & Michael